other books by the Trobisches:
Better Is Your Love Than Wine
I Loved a Girl
I Married You
The Joy of Being a Woman
Living with Unfulfilled Desires
Love Is a Feeling to Be Learned
Love Yourself
My Beautiful Feeling
On Our Way Rejoicing

booklets by Walter Trobisch:
Martin Luther's Quiet Time
Spiritual Dryness

Further information about the Ovulation Method of Natural Family Planning can be obtained from:

O. M. Centre
M. M. M. Hospital
P. O. Box 20
Ondo, Ondo State
Nigeria

Couple to Couple League
P. O. Box 11084
3614 Glenmore Ave.
Cincinnati, Ohio 45211
U. S. A.

N. F. P. Council of Victoria
86 Wellington Parade
East Melbourne
Victoria 3002
Australia

Teaching material on the Ovulation Method can be purchased from:

The Human Life Foundation
1511 K Street N. W.
Washington D. C. 20005
U. S. A.

The ATLAS OF THE OVULATION METHOD written by Drs. John and Evelyn Billings can be ordered from:

Advocate Press Pty. Ltd.
143—151 A. Beckett St.
Melbourne 3000
Australia

A
BABY
Just Now?
Walter Trobisch

InterVarsity Press
Downers Grove
Illinois 60515

InterVarsity Press is the book-publishing division of Inter-Varsity Christian Fellowship, a student movement active on campus at hundreds of universities, colleges and schools of nursing. For information about local and regional activities, write IVCF, 233 Langdon St., Madison, WI 53703.

Originally published under the title Please Help Me! Please Love Me!

Distributed in Canada through InterVarsity Press, 1875 Leslie St., Unit 10, Don Mills, Ontario M3B 2M5, Canada.

ISBN 0-87784-849-1

Printed in the United States of America

Library of Congress Cataloging in Publication Data
Trobisch, Walter.
   A baby just now?
   Ed. for 1970 published under title: Please help me!
Please love me!
   1.   Birth control–Religious aspects.   I.   Title.
HQ766.2.T76   1980   261.8'3666   80-17213
ISBN 0-87784-849-1

14	13	12	11	10	9	8	7	6	5	4	3	2	1
91	90	89	88	87	86	85	84	83	82	81	80		

When Joseph first wrote to me and complained about his „disobedient" wife, I did not know that our correspondence would end up in such a lengthy discussion about the problems connected with family planning. While we were searching for answer, we became more and more aware of the relationship between marital happiness and the success in spacing one's children, preventing or favouring conception — as God guides.

Joseph is an African. But his problems are basically the same as in any other part of the world. Perhaps they are more sharply focused because certain African customs and traditions may make it harder for Joseph to find solutions than for others who belong to another culture. But just for this reason our correspondence may prove helpful to many.

As you will see, the idea of publishing part of our correspondence occurred to both of us while we were writing. Still the advice I have given to Joseph is, in the first place, meant for him alone in his specific situation. Please don't make the mistake of generalizing it and misunderstanding my suggestions as a general law valid for everyone.

This book does not attempt to give answer for everyone everywhere. But one thing it does want to teach: *The seeking of God's will by both husband and wife together is vitally important to family planning. It is the basic condition for any answer to this great human problem.*

Walter Trobisch

Lichtenberg 6
A-4880 St. Georgen
Austria

Sir,

I have heard about your work and therefore I take the liberty to write to you and to place my case before you. Here is my problem: I am 24 years old. Three years ago I was married to a 15-year-old person. But now this person does not want to obey me any more.

I am a teacher and have ten years of schooling. My wife stopped after her sixth year. I purposely did not choose someone who had reached a higher level of education than I had. I intended to train my wife for life: to drill her for cleanliness as a housewife and to raise her for marriage as a spouse. In short, she should become exactly as I wanted her to be.

At the beginning of our marriage it worked somehow. But during the last year she did not satisfy me any more. Regardless of what I command her to do, she never does it. If I tell her something, she refuses. If I insist, we start to quarrel even to the point of fighting.

Sometimes we make peace and try to start

anew. But it lasts only for one day. Then we fall back into quarrelling. My wife gets angry very easily. Sometimes she even throws our household out of the window. The only thing she seems to enjoy is jealousy.

I might also mention that God blessed us with a child who is already one year and one month old.

I have confidence in you and hope that whatever you tell me will serve as a remedy to our sick marriage.

Joseph

January 28

Dear Mr. Joseph,

Thank you very much for your letter and also for your confidence. I wish I could pay you a visit. Then it would be easier for me to find the root of your trouble. I am afraid it will be hard for me to help by letter-writing alone, but I shall try my best.

Your wife was too young when you married her. This is certainly one of the reason for your difficulties. At 15, a girl is still a child. When she is 18, she is a young woman. The change she goes through between 15 and 18 is tremendous. For a girl these are the most important years of maturing. Not only does her body change, but also her spirit, her character and her emotions. At 18, a girl is an entirely different person than she was at 15, especially if she has become a mother in the meantime, as is the case with your wife.

May I speak frankly? I am afraid that when you married her you did not look for a wife, but more or less for a daughter, perhaps even a maid. You did not plan so much to become a husband to her as you did to become a father or even an employer.

The verbs you use when describing your relationship to her are very revealing: „to train", „to drill", „to raise". Do you know that one could use these verbs also for an animal?

You planned to educate her as you educate your students in class, to dominate her as a superior dominates someone in an inferior position. Instead of a marriage partner you were looking for a servant.

It is hard for me to judge from this distance, but my impression is that your wife rebels against being treated like a servant. She wants to be treated as an equal partner.

God loves your wife as much as he loves you. Both of you are equal in his eyes. God has a plan for you as well as for your wife. He has given unique gifts to your wife and he wants her to make use of them. He wants her talents and skills to unfold just as a flower unfolds from a bud. It is your task to help her become what G o d wants her to be, not what y o u want her to be.

Her jealousy shows that she loves you, but that she cannot fully trust you. This may be a reflection of the fact that you do not trust her either. As soon as she feels that you have confidence in her, she may be more cooperative.

Marriage is like the echo in the forest. What you call out will come back to you.

If you say that she does not satisfy you, you must ask yourself: „Do I satisfy her?" If you complain that she does not have confidence in you, you must ask yourself: „Do I have confidence in her?" If you criticize her for not obeying and serving you, you must ask yourself: „Do I obey and serve her?"

If you feel she hinders you from becoming what God wants you to be, then you must ask yourself: "Do I give her a chance to become what God wants h e r to be?"

There is one expression in your letter which I did not understand. You say that your wife "throws the household out of the window". Do you mean that she literally throws the dishes out into the street?

Let me share this last thought with you. I was struck by the fact that your quarrelling started about the time your child was born, approximately one year ago. How long is the period of lactation in your tribe when you abstain from sex relations with your wife?

You see it is not God's will for a married couple to abstain from physical union for too long a time.

Sharing and meeting each other's sexual needs is so important that the apostle Paul advises against prolonged abstinence: "Do not refuse one another except perhaps by agreement for a season, that you may devote yourselves to prayer; but then come together again, lest Satan tempt you through lack of self-control."

My question is this: Could it be that your quarrelling is a result of such a temptation and that there is a sexual problem behind it?

Feel free not to answer this question if it embarrasses you too much. I just have to ask this question because its answer may help me to find the "remedy for your sick marriage".

February 15

Dear Pastor T.,

I can't express the joy caused by your letter. It is as if you had lived right among us. Since your letter came, the troubled sea of our marriage has already calmed down. I do not know how to thank you, for I am sure that you have already found the reason our marriage is sick.

It is just as you assumed. In my tribe we abstain from sex relations for two years after the birth of a baby. This is because of certain superstitions of our ancestors. They say that sex relations with a woman who has a small child will endanger the life of her baby.

This custom is embodied in us and we are afraid we will lose the baby if we have intercourse with the mother as long as she breast-feeds it. She does that until the baby starts to walk.

They also say that boys die easier than girls — and our child is a boy. My father-in-law emphasized that fact to me after our boy was born. Therefore for fear that we cause his death we abstained from intercourse for several months.

But it was hard, especially for me. In former times when polygamy still reigned in our society, I guess it must have been easier to follow this custom. But I despise polygamy as do most young men of my generation. It is something which belongs to the past. In any case, even if I wanted to take a second wife, it would be impossible for me because of financial reasons.

My wife knows that many husbands commit adultery in such a situation. As a church elder and as a teacher at a church school I would not even think of going to a prostitute. Still my wife suspects it and this makes her distrustful and jealous.

To whom could I have turned to solve my problem? One day I met a friend who advised me to use a method which I felt was vulgar. He told me that it is the sperm inside the woman's body which kills the baby, because it mixes with the milk. But if I would withdraw and shed the sperm outside of my wife's body, intercourse would not be dangerous for our baby.

Something in me rebelled against this, but since I felt that my wife and I were gradually drifting apart as long as we abstained from sex relations, I tried it. That's the way we do it at present. It has given me some release, but it has not helped our marriage.

There are many things which I do not understand. It seems to me that my wife is not satisfied if I ejaculate outside of her body. Could it be that the sperm has another quality or effect when it is not used for the purpose of procreation? Is it possible that only sperm inside my wife's body contributes to sexual harmony?

I would be very grateful to you if you could clarify my thinking on these questions.

P. S. "Throwing the household out of the window" is an expression in our language for gossiping and slander. My wife started to tell our secrets to the other women in the village, and that makes me feel terribly embarrassed. But sometimes in an outbreak of anger she actually breaks plates and cups and throws them on the earth and toward the wall.

February 27

Dear Joseph,

I am so glad that my question did not hurt you, but rather caused you to give me a full picture of the situation. I can well understand now why your wife rebels.

13

You are really in a dilemma. On one hand you do not want to become polygamous and on the other hand you want to follow a custom which presupposes a polygamous society.

The reasoning behind this custom is not entirely wrong though. Since there was neither fresh nor powdered milk available in your tribe, babies had to be breastfed, usually for about two years. If the mother got pregnant before that and could not nurse her baby, the baby could easily have died.

It is also true that girls are more resistant to disease than boys. That explains the statement of your father-in-law.

This high rate of infant mortality in former times, however, was not caused by intercourse. The sperm does not mix with the milk. This is a biological impossibility. Those babies probably died because of an inadequate diet when their mothers' milk supply dried up due to another pregnancy.

Your ancestors observed correctly that couples who had intercourse before their baby was weaned were more apt to lose it. Their conclusion was that abstaining from intercourse gives the baby a better chance to survive. I know some other tribes where this period of abstention lasts for three years. But then — as you say — husband and wife drift apart gradually. A period of abstention of six weeks before and after the birth is all right, but in no case is it advisable to abstain from marital relations for two or even three years.

You are right: It must have been easier when a man had more than one wife. From this point of view one could say that polygamy was the traditional African way of "conception control". It helped the women to space their children.

You rule out polygamy for yourself for emotional and financial reason — and I am the last one who wants to contradict you. In addition to the reasons which you give, let me briefly mention here that the Bible points out very soberly and realistically the disadvantages of polygamy. Genesis 26 says that it makes life bitter (v. 35), Genesis 29 that it causes rivalry (v. 30) and hatred (v. 31), Genesis 30 that it leads to envy (v. 1), anger (v. 2) and wrestling and fighting (v. 8). Genesis 37 stresses the effect of polygamy on the children: favoritism and injustice (v. 3), hostility (v. 4), jealousy (v. 4) and finally murder (v. 18).

I do not know of a single passage in the Bible where polygamy is not mentioned under a negative aspect.

Also I am glad that you reject prostitution as well. I believe that prostitution is the main reason for so many childless marriages in Africa. Men who sleep with prostitutes can easily catch a venereal disease, infect their wives and cause them to become sterile.

In fact, many of the so-called prostitutes in African towns are such sterile women, who were abandoned by their husbands because they could not bear children. If they have a venereal disease, they pass it on to their customers who in turn may make their own wives barren. Then the men leave these wives because of their barrenness and many of the women have no other choice except to earn their living through prostitution.

It is really a vicious circle. I once heard an African judge say, „Whoever sleeps with a prostitute commits a criminal act against his own people. It is comparable to high treason." I don't think he exaggerated.

Yes, indeed: To whom could you have turned? Formerly you would have consulted with the elders of your tribe, but now you are in a different situation unknown to them. I am afraid that your church also just left you with a negative message, saying that polygamy is wrong and prostitution is sinful. What you needed was positive advice on how to space your children in a monogamous marriage.

The method which your friend advised is called "coitus interruptus" or more commonly "being careful". It consists in the withdrawal of the penis from the vagina before ejaculation occurs.

Let me simply quote what the Medical Handbook of the International Planned Parenthood Federation says about the disadvantages of this method:

> Various emotional disturbances in the form of anxiety in both the male and the female partner are said to be produced by the prolonged and

*continued use of this method. The female is
constantly in fear that the male will not withdraw
in time, and the male must be in a continued
state of vigilance in order to gauge the right
moment for separation. Thus one of the desirable
features of intercourse, complete freedom from
anxiety, is lost, and replaced by unavoidable
tension. This may possibly result in impotence
in the male, frigidity in the female, or a state of
nervous tension in either.*[1]

Now you know why you quarrel and also why
your wife "throws the household out of the window" by word of mouth or by action. Both of
you are in a permanent state of nervous tension.

The name "interrupted intercourse" is mislead-
ing. Actually intercourse is not interrupted in
order to be continued later on, but it is broken
off. Since it takes much longer for a woman to
reach her climax, usually only the male partner
experiences a sort of satisfaction, while the female partner remains tense and unsatisfied. It is
not the lack of sperm which leaves her unsatisfied, but the lack of time, connected with fear
and worry.

The inabiliy to relax due to congestion may
actually cause her abdominal pain and in the long
run she may develop a loathsome and disgusting
feeling against everything sexual.

Consciously or unconsciously she blames you

1) I. P. P. F. Medical Handbook "Contraception",
1967, p. 49, 1810 Tower Regent St., London, S. W. I, England.

17

for it and develops a negative attitude against you. She does not feel loved but exploited. Through her "disobedience" she protests against this exploitation. By breaking cups and plates she tries to find release from tension.

But, Joseph, this means that her disobedience is basically a cry for help. She tries to call your attention to her need. What she really wants to say is: "Please help me! Please love me!"

I would strongly advise you to choose another method for preventing conception, especially since "coitus abruptus", as I prefer to call it, is not a safe method either. Not only can the moment of withdrawal be easily missed, but it is also possible that sperm may be present in the small amount of pre-ejaculation moisture at the tip of the erect penis. Therefore any movement of the penis in the vagina automatically causes this moisture and the sperm to be deposited on the vaginal wall. Pregnancies have even occurred following movements of the penis against the moist part of the vulva without actual penetration or ejaculation.

In your case I would advise you to turn to "Natural Family Planning" (NFP), which means to live in harmony with the biological laws according to which you were created.

Dear Pastor T.,

The last paragraphs of your letter of February 27th leave me dumbfounded. I am quite sure that you are right in the analysis of our problem. So is my wife. I let Jeannette read your letter and while she was reading it, she sometimes giggled with laughter. That's the way she always does when something strikes her.

We agree that the method of birth control which we have been using is responsible for lots of our trouble.

Your diagnosis is good, but I do not understand your alternative. I simply do not know what you mean by "Natural Family Planning". What are those laws according to which we were created? Since, as a teacher, I have more education than the average man in my country, I guess I am not alone in this ignorance. Our district pastor does not know what it is either. Sex education was not a part of the highly praised western education which we received.

There is a Protestant mission station not far from here. I know the missionary families quite well. Some get a child almost every year and seem to have no feeding problem. Others get them in regular intervals of two years. How do they manage that? What kind of magic do they have? Why do they never talk to us Africans about the methods of birth control which they use?

Dear Joseph,

You stung my missionary conscience. I believe that you are right in your criticism.

I agree, it is unkind and merciless if missionaries discourage polygamy, but keep silent about other methods of conception control. No, my dear friend, they do not have any "magic". They solve their feeding problem with the help of powdered milk and if they want advice for spacing their children, their missionary doctor will provide them with everything they need.

Thank you for not hiding your ignorance. It was an eye-opener to me. What a tremendous task of giving out information lies before us! When will schools in Africa start to include sex education in their schedules?

But before I start explaining what I meant by Natural Family Planning let's get our terms straight. You will notice that I did not use the expression "birth control" in our correspondence. That was intentional, because the term "birth control" conceives of birth as the beginning of life. Consequently a willful abortion could also then be justified as a means of " birth control".

I prefer to use the term "conception control" because it sees the fecundation of the female ovum by the male seed as the beginning of life. Every destruction of this new life — in other words, every intentional abortion — is murder.

Natural Family Planning means simply to abstain from intercourse during the fertile days in a woman's menstrual cycle.

A woman can only conceive during the time when the egg cell or ovum separates from the ovary. This process is called ovulation. If the ovum is not met by a male sperm shortly after ovulation, no fertilization takes place and the woman experiences a slight bleeding about two weeks later, as if the womb were shedding "tears of disappointment". We say then a woman has "her period" or "her days" or "she menstruates."

You can control conception by adjusting intercourse to the natural rhythm of a woman's body. This explains the name „Natural Family Planning". If a couple abstains from intercourse during the time of ovulation, which is her fertile time, no conception can take place.

I suggest this method to you because I feel that it would ease the tenseness of your wife and give her a better chance to find satisfaction by experiencing an orgasm.

By the way, do you know what made me most happy about your last letter? The fact that you shared it with your wife! This means that you have stopped treating her as a "daughter" and started to recognize her as an adult and as a partner. Tell her that she may write to me too, if she cares to.

Dear Pastor T.,

Thank you for your letter. Could you give me permission to copy some paragraphs and pass it on to friends who have similar problems? I know quite af few who would be very grateful for this help.

However, if I do this then my students could also get a hold of it and I am afraid that they would abuse this knowledge, applying it to pre-marital relations. How could I avoid this?

Some months ago we had to send a girl away from school because she was pregnant. When I questioned her, she claimed that she was sure that intercourse had occurred on her "safe days", which she said were the days halfway between two periods. She thought she could only conceive immediately before or following her period.

So you see, our students have some kind of knowledge of these things, but very often it is incorrect. I am sorry that at that time I was unable to correct her error.

My question is, if I had already known what you explained to me in your last letter, should I have told her? Wouldn't I have led her into temptation? And could she have been sure that the days which you describe are absolutely safe?

My wife also has a question. I enclose her note:

Good morning, Pastor. This is Jeannette writing.

I read your letters to Joseph. I would also like to ask you a question.

I am very interested in your suggestion that we have no intercourse when the ovum is leaving the ovary. But my question is: How can I know? Do I feel this? Are there signs to help me recognize when ovulation takes place?

July 6

Dear Joseph and Jeannette,

You did not put enough stamps on your last letter and it went by surface mail. Because of this I am very sorry that I was not able to answer your important question sooner.

Let us take „ladies first". Thank you, Jeannette, for your note. Yes, there are symptoms to help you recognize your time of ovulation. Perhaps you have noticed that just after your menstrual bleeding has finished, there are a few days of dryness at the vaginal opening. When this dryness changes to a feeling of wetness you will know that your fertile time is beginning. Then for two or three days you will notice a transparent, stretchy fluid, very similar to raw egg - white at the mouth of the vagina. This is the symptom or sign that ovulation is taking place. This fluid is called "cervical mucus" and your body produces it in order to help your husband's semen enter into the womb and meet the ovum.

If you want to have a baby, then you would have to unite during the days when you see this cervical mucus. If you do not want to have a baby just yet, then you should not have intercourse during these days p l u s three days after the slippery egg-white mucus has stopped completely. It is necessary to wait for three days in order to be sure that the ovum is no longer living. Otherwise conception could still take place.

After that, the infertile time of your cycle begins and you are not able to conceive until the fertile time of your next cycle. Some women in your country describe this fertile-type of mucus as being similar to the soup of gumbo which you cook — stretchy and quite clear. You can examine the mucus on two leaves, or with your fingers, testing it to see if it will stretch. Some women think when they see this symptom that they are sick. On the contrary, this is a sign of good health.

Now back to Joseph's questions. I am glad you raised the problem of premarital relations. The premarital situation and the marital situation are different. Usually when methods of conception control are discussed, the two situations are not kept apart properly. What is applicable in a marital situation is not applicable in the same way in a premarital situation.

This is especially true about Natural Family Planning. For premarital intercourse it is almost useless as a safeguard against an unwanted pregnancy. The boy would have to believe the girl when she says that she is "safe". How can he be sure that she tells him the truth as in the case of your student? And even if she does know the truth, what guarantee does he have that she has interpreted this symptom correctly?

Girls who give themselves easily before marriage are usually not very trustworthy, disciplined, conscientious and — by the way — not very intelligent either. Natural Family Planning needs a high measure of discipline, conscientiousness and intelligence. Girls who use NFP and live consciously in harmony with their cycle are automatically trained in these qualities. This is, in turn, their best protection against indulging in premarital sex.

Does knowledge lead into temptation? Yes, it does, if it is abused. I do not think that there is any means to prevent the abuse of knowledge. If we refuse to give true knowledge, false knowledge will spread. The case of your girl student illustrates this in a striking way.

Those who want to have premarital relations will have them anyway, whether or not we give out information. But by giving correct information we may save some of these young people from disasters and from destroying their lives.

So much depends upon the atmosphere in which such knowledge is conveyed. When talking to unmarried teenagers, you must emphasize that there is no "absolutely safe" method of conception control, except for one. This is the word "No". If your students feel that you stand behind your words with your action and your own conduct of life, they will readily accept your advice. Reliable and trustworthy information may prevent them from experimenting themselves with disastrous results. Once they are married and away from you, they will remember you gratefully.

September 20

Dear Pastor T.,

During vacation I went to my home village. This is why it has taken me until now to answer your letter of July 6th.

Again when I read it, I thought of so many others who need such information. The idea is quite widespread here that it is the third day after her period when a woman can conceive. But I have no time to copy your letter so often. Could you help me to mimeograph it or even print it?

This is only to tell you how thankful we were for your explanation. Still, I have to confess to you, dear Pastor T., that we are not too happy. We tried now for half a year to watch symptoms, but it often happens that on the infertile days, when we could unite, we are hindered by some outward disturbance.

On the other hand, during the fertile days, when we shouldn't come together, we would like to and also circumstances would allow it. It's really tricky.

This brings up another handicap. As a European it will be hard for you to understand this. For us Africans it's very hard to talk about these things. I simply cannot bring it across my lips to ask Jeannette about her mucus symptoms nor is she able to tell me. So I am never sure whether she forgot to watch for this sign of fertility.

True, my wife is less jealous, but we still have problems with this method.

What has helped us most is to share your letters. The fact that she knows that I know how she feels and cares about it has made our marriage more peaceful.

I heard that a mother can't conceive as long as she breastfeeds her baby. Is that true?

I read in a magazine that millions of American women take the so-called "anti-baby pills". What do the pills do? Kill the baby? What do you think about them? Can it be sinful to prevent conception? What is God's will about family planning?

October 6

Dear Joseph,

I am glad that we are in contact again and that you share your experiences with me so frankly.

What you have heard is right. Normally a woman does not menstruate as long as she breastfeeds her child c o m p l e t e l y. This is because she has no ovulation and consequently she cannot conceive. Many doctors believe that it is the stimulus of the sucking of the baby which prevents ovulation. However, it is not true that a woman cannot become pregnant as long as she is nursing a baby, although it is extremely unusual before the first menstrual period if she is completely nursing her baby. The average nursing mother will not have a period for several months after giving birth. When she does begin to have menstrual periods, in most cases at least one and often several of these will be without ovulation. That is why it is very important for a breast-feeding mother to notice the return of the mucus sign which means she can conceive again.

You ask about God's will about family planning. It is, above all, a matter of conscience. It is the motive which counts before God, not the method or the means.

If a couple does not want to have children because of selfish reasons (for example, material greed, love of luxury or simply laziness), then any kind of conception control is sinful.

If, on the other hand, a new pregnancy would endanger the mother's or the baby's life, it would be sinful not to use conception control. A father whose income is small and who already has five or six children whom he wants to give a fairly good education may want to limit the number of his children for this reason. He may do so with a good conscience before God, because his motive is unselfish.

The important thing is that father and mother together make such a decision. Together they have to examine their consciences before God as to their motive. Together they are responsible to God. This is what we call "responsible parenthood".

Now a word about the so-called "anti-baby-pill". The name "anti-baby pill" is awkward. No baby is killed. What the pill does is hinder ovulation. As long as a woman takes these pills, no ovum is released from the ovary. Consequently, fertilization cannot take place.

That means that a couple can have intercourse on any day between the periods without restriction. Whether this makes marriages happier is a disputed question. Some couples feel that it takes the spice out of their relations and makes them monotonous when they could have them every day. The increased sexual demands are too great for a number of marriage partners, who then suffer from frigidity or impotence. Especially the wife may complain of becoming "depersonalized". She may feel that she has degenerated into a sexual object instead of being an equal partner in married love. Somehow intervals make intimate relations more attractive and the happiness of loving is refreshed and intensified.

But as far as effectiveness goes, the pill is as effective as Natural Family Planning. However, there is one important hitch to this effectiveness: between the menstrual periods one pill must be taken every day for 21 days. Otherwise the effectiveness cannot be guaranteed.

Consequently — and this is what you have to tell your teenage girls — it is useless for a girl to take one pill along with her when going on a date and then swallow it quickly just in case.

Again we have to distinguish between marital and premarital use of this method. In premarital situations the pill cannot be considered an effective method. The boy who has dated an unmarried girl would have to believe her if she claims to have taken her pills every day. Effectiveness depends upon whether she tells the truth or not.

As I said before, "easy" girls are not usually very conscientious and the conscientious girls with high moral standards would most likely agree with the American girl who said: "If I would take pills regularly, calculatingly, in anticipation of a possible sex adventure, I would feel like a prostitute."

More and more doctors caution young girls especially from taking pills, because it can have a negative effect on a girl's organism and change the normal delicate balance of her hormones. In any case, pills must be prescribed by a medical doctor and medical supervision is imperative, especially since we still have very little knowledge about the after-effects in later years. Because I assumed that such supervision is difficult in your village, I did not advise you to use this method. The pills are also quite expensive.

In many cases as soon as a woman stops taking the pills, her ability to conceive is especially great and many unwanted pregnancies occur during the first months after she stops.

Or on the contrary, the normal release of egg cells may be hindered when a woman quits taking the pills and she may be sterile for a longer time.

If you decide to use this method I would advise you, as the husband, to keep the pills and give one to your wife every day. In this way you also take a share of the responsibility and you cannot blame Jeannette for being forgetful in case of an unintended pregnancy.

You have to decide. But in order to decide you have to talk. I know that it is difficult, but I am afraid you will have to learn. It is impossible to live a marriage without talking to each other. Sharing is the secret of marriage.

October 18

Dear Pastor T.,

When your last letter arrived I was not at home. But Jeannette was so eager to read it that she opened it, though it was addressed to me. Was that right?

You said that the secret of marriage is sharing. Does this mean that husband and wife are allowed to open each other's mail? I must say that I did not like it.

So for the first time since we started to correspond with you, we again had a little disagreement. On the other hand, I must say that sharing your letters has helped us a great deal to talk to each other even about sexual matters. I think you are right when you say that Jeannette's "disobedience" was just a way of saying that she wanted to be listened to, understood and cared for.

Jeannette refuses absolutely to take pills. She says it would give her the feeling of being poisoned even if she knows that they contain no poison. She has an instinctive horror of such pills.

Most of us Africans are much more open to watching natural symptoms than to using artificial means.

On the other hand, Jeannette and I are not yet friends with the idea of periodical abstention. So our basic problem is not yet solved. We do not want another baby just yet. Powdered milk is too expensive for us and not available here in the village anyway. We are afraid to use fresh milk because our children die if they drink it. I know that the children of the missionaries don't get sick from it, but ours do.

The other day we heard about a woman who already has eight children. She went to a dispensary about 50 miles from here. There a nurse put something into her body which looked like a little snake. She said that this would prevent conception and not do any harm. Have you ever heard about such a thing?

November 1

Dear Joseph and Jeannette,

Opening each other's mail is a delicate problem. I shall address my letters from now on to both of you. I should have done that already with my last letter because it was definitely meant for both of you.

Sharing does not mean sneaking. Normally, I would say, each one should open his own mail, even if it is only for the joy of opening a letter! But it should be a matter of course that one shares gladly one's own mail with the marriage partner, talks about it and decides together what to answer. You have already experienced how much sharing the mail helps towards peace and understanding.

Sharing is especially important in order to avoid mistrust and jealousy when correspondence takes place with the opposite sex.

A pastor's mail is definitely an exception. He may receive confidential letters which he is not allowed to share with anyone, not even with his wife. This puts the marriage of a pastor to an especially hard test. If he has a wife who does not understand this, she can wreck his ministry — and his marriage at the same time.

I have made an agreement with my wife — who also receives confidential letters — that we never open each other's mail. Normally we share it. But if one of us does not feel free to share a letter, the other one does not ask any questions about it. This is only possible, of course, if full and complete confidence reigns between husband and wife.

I am happy that you both have read my last letter and talked about it. Joseph, please do not try to persuade Jeannette to take pills she does not want to. If she has an aversion against them, just this alone would greatly hinder her achieving sexual fulfillment. A woman who feels "poisoned" does not enjoy sex.

However, I disagree with you entirely about fresh milk. The missionaries boil their milk before drinking it. This is the reason why their children do not get sick. Your children would not either. On the contrary, they would thrive.

May I say frankly, if you only want to wait to have another baby because you refuse to boil your milk, this is not reason enough to practice conception control.

The thing that was inserted in the woman you mentioned was an "intrauterine device" (I. U. D). This is no "snake", but a plastic spiral or sling which is placed inside the uterus, or womb, to avoid the implantation of the fertilized ovum.

This brings up a theological question connected with this method. The question is: "When does life begin?" If we claim that life begins in the moment when the sperm unites with the ovum, it would mean that the I. U. D.'s produce a pre-clinical abortion. I know many people whose conscience does not allow them to use this method for this reason.

From the medical point of view the tender tissues of the uterus are in danger of infection through the presence of the I. U. D., a foreign body in the womb. Certain side effects such as bleeding, pain, and sometimes perforation of the uterus cannot be entirely avoided.

There is also the possiblity that an I. U. D. is spontaneously expelled especially during a menstrual period. If the woman doesn't notice this, then conception usually follows.

In passing, let me mention a few other devices here. Sooner or later you may be asked about them and I want you to be informed.

In some countries, a three-month injection has been given to women to prevent pregnancy. This is very dangerous and can cause permanent damage to a woman's reproductive system.

Another method consists of covering the mouth of the uterus in order to prevent semen from entering. The device used for this purpose is called a diaphragm. A doctor's advice is necessary for fitting it. Even then, a diaphragm does not offer much security except in combination with a sperm-killing ointment. If it is not inserted properly, it is useless.

Flooding the vagina with water after coitus — the so-called "douches" — cannot be effective, since sperms can reach the cervix within 90 seconds of ejaculation.

Joseph, I feel like almost apologizing to you for writing you all this. I certainly didn't think, when you wrote me the first time, that our correspondence would end up in such a lengthy discussion of contraceptive methods. But if you think of using a mechanical device at all, I would think of something rather harmless, the condom.

I mean the rubber sheath which completely covers the male organ like the finger of a glove. The seminal fluid is caught in it and cannot enter the vagina.

However during the time of the fertile days it is not very reliable to prevent conception, while during the infertile days you would not need it.

November 16

Dear Pastor T.,

Before I tell you what I think about condoms, I would like to ask some general questions about "conception control".

Jeannette took your letter to one of her friends who is the mother of fourteen children. She came back home with a whole bag of questions which we were unable to answer.

Jeannette's friend claims that the Bible does not say anything about contraceptives. She says that God gave Adam and Eve the commandment, "Be fruitful and multiply and fill the earth". Therefore the use of any contraceptives, even observing the infertile days, would be against God's will. It would be sinful to have intercourse if you did not intend to produce offspring. One should not interfere with the course of nature, but rather leave everything entirely in God's hand and trust him and believe him.

We did not know how to answer her. She is a very pious woman and really believes in the Bible.

When you have answered, I shall tell you my story about the rubber sheath.

Dear Joseph and Jeannette,

Now you turn tables!

Remember, it was not I who advised you to wait with another child! You had made this decision without me, long before you wrote to me the first time. However, the method which you had used to space your children had disturbed the harmony of your marriage. This was the reason why we discussed other methods which would be less disturbing.

I think it is good that you bring up the basic question: Is conception control in harmony at all with the will of God? What does the Bible say about it?

The Bible does not make any direct statement about conception control. In this, your wife's friend is right. Neither is any specific method mentioned in the Bible. This is the more surprising since certain methods were already known and practiced during the times when the Bible was written.

The Bible stresses again and again that children are a blessing of God and a source of joy: "Children are an heritage of the Lord, and the fruit of the womb is his reward" (Ps. 127 : 3).

According to divine will, sexual union and

procreation are closely related to each other. The fact that there is no ideal method of conception control is a silent testimony to this truth. Every method has its disadvantages and disturbs the fellowship of the lovers in one way or the other. To ignore entirely the deep connection between the sex act and offspring — as it is done in prostitution for instance — is certainly sinful.

However, the Bible does not consider procreation as the only purpose of the sex act. Your wife's friend is mistaken here. Both the Old and the New Testament testify that sexual union is a legitimate expression of marital love, even if the production of children is neither achieved nor intended. Barrenness is never recognized in the Bible as a reason for divorce. A marriage remains a marriage even without children. The love between husband and wife as expressed by sexual union has the promise of fulfillment in itself.

Therefore the Bible can speak about this love without mentioning children. In Proverbs 31, you find a twenty-five verse description of a good housewife. Only one of these twenty-five verses mentions children. This shows that in Israel a woman was much more than just a means to produce offspring or a sort of breeding machine.

In Genesis 29, you can read about the love of Jacob and Rachel and in I Samuel 18 and 19 about David's love to Michal without there being a question of children. The same is true about the Song of Solomon.

In Genesis 2 : 18, God says to Adam, "It is not good that the man should be alone; I will make a helper fit for him." This means that according to the Bible, the woman is not essentially a womb, a sort of well-equipped incubator, but an equivalent to man as his suitable, corresponding partner complementing him and forming with him a new entity.

The Bible praises this entity, this total fellowship of body, mind and soul with the phrase, "they become one flesh" (Gen. 2 : 24).

Children are not mentioned. The emphasis is on the dignity of the woman, not on procreation. This is especially true in the New Testament where Jesus gave a new dignity to the wife by forbidding divorce. There is no commandment about procreation in the New Testament. Parenthood is a free gift of God's goodness, but childlessness is no shame.

When the apostle Paul talks about the physical fellowship between husband and wife in I Corinthians 7 : 3, the question of children doesn't even enter in. When he explains the relationship between husband and wife in marriage in Ephesians 5, children aren't mentioned either.[1]

To sum it up, according to the biblical testimony as a whole, the fellowship of love in marriage has its own dignity — apart from the question of children.

1) See I L o v e d a G i r l, letter of August 3rd.

If this is true, then it is a logical conclusion that man has to make a decision about the question of children. It is not an automatic, mechanical process. To "leave nature to its course" is not at all the same as "leaving it entirely in God's hand". This is not biblical thinking! According to the Bible, nature belongs to this world which has fallen out of God's hand. Therefore not "to interfere with nature" can be against God's will. Uncontrolled fertility can be destructive and a way to worship and serve "the creature rather than the Creator" (Rom 1 : 25). Therefore it is biblical for the Philippine Independent Church to state: "The irresponsible procreation of children can be sinful".

If the mother of fourteen children who talked to Jeannette has a sense of humor, you can tell her that when God commanded man to "fill the earth" he did not mean that she should do it all by herself.

Seriously though, since you say she "really believes in the Bible", you should challenge her to quote the verse in full. That which she has quoted to Jeannette is just the first half of the blessing which God gave to Adam and Eve. The full verse reads as follows:

"And God blessed them, and said to them: Be fruitful and multiply, and fill the earth and subdue it; and have dominion over the fish of the sea and over the birds of the air and over every living thing that moves upon the earth " (Gen. 1 : 28).

What I have dominion over, I am responsible for. If I am put in the driver's seat and given dominion over a car, I am responsible for steering it. A statesman who has dominion over a nation is responsible for the course it takes. A director who has dominion over a factory is responsible for its output. If man is given dominion over "every living being" it means that as father and mother, he is responsible for the use of his procreative powers.

Therefore I prefer to speak about "responsible parenthood" rather than about "conception control" or even "birth control".

In view of the fact that the population of the earth will have reached the number of 6.3 milliards by the year 2000, some have raised the question whether the commandment "fill the earth" is not already fulfilled. Is not the task of subduing the earth endangered by overfilling it?

In any case, the task of man is not multiplication, but dominion; not nature, but culture.

Therefore man is responsible for the way in which the commandment "Be fruitful and multiply" is carried out. It is an abuse to interpret this commandment as an invitation to irresponsible procreation and to find in it an excuse for not making a decision.

If you want to give Jeannette's friend a Bible verse as the basis for responsible parenthood, then give her I Timothy 5 : 8: "If any one does not provide for his relatives, and especially for his own family, he has disowned the faith and is worse than an unbeliever."

Dear Pastor T.,

I must have asked you a very difficult question in order for you to write such a long letter! Please be assured that it is worth the effort. The whole neighbourhood is already participating in our conversation and your letters go from hand to hand.

If I understand you correctly, you draw your conclusions for "responsible parenthood" from the biblical concept of marriage in general. You say that because procreation is not the only purpose of the sex act, man has freedom and the obligation of making a decision about offspring. But you arrive there only by way of conclusion.

Therefore Jeannette's friend, the Bible-believing woman with fourteen children, was not at all convinced. She still claims that there is no commandment in the Bible to use contraceptives and neither is there any advice about which means or methods to use.

The basic question as I see it is now: "A r e w e p e r m i t t e d t o d o s o m e t h i n g w h i c h G o d h a s n o t e x p r e s s l y c o m-m a n d e d?"

The woman also quoted the story of Onan in Genesis 38 : 9, 10 and maintained that God punished Onan by death because he prevented the procreation of offspring by spilling his seed on the ground.

She concluded that the practice of any means of contraception is sinful. I have never read this passage from this point of view. I always thought that it talked about masturbation. Is the woman's interpretation right?

I am not clear about these things. This brings up the story about the condom. Just because I am not clear, I probably made a mistake the other day in class.

One of my students had brought such a rubber sheath along into the classroom. He claimed that he had found it under a tree and asked me innocently what it was.

Of course, he just wanted to embarrass me, and all the students — boys and girls — giggled. Therefore I didn't give him any answer but punished him severely. I am not sure whether this was the right reaction.

I was wondering all the time why you had never mentioned condoms in our correspondence. Frankly, I cannot imagine myself going into a pharmacy and asking for them, especially if a woman waits on me. This could spoil my reputation as a teacher and my testimony as a Christian. In our country condoms are thought of as items to be used with prostitutes only as a prevention against venereal disease.

Well, I am afraid you will have to write another long letter. Thanks in advance . . .

Dear Joseph and Jeannette,

I am sorry that I wasn't able to answer sooner. Now that Christmas is over, I have more time to think about your important questions.

Are we permitted to do something which God has not expressly commanded?

I suppose you wash yourself with soap and water every morning and you brush your teeth. I am sure you will not find any Bible verse where this is "expressly commanded" and still you are entirely in accordance with the will of God by doing it. How do you know? By way of conclusion!

We confess in our Creed, "I believe in God the Father Almighty, Maker of heaven and earth." This means that our physical life is entrusted to us by God. We are responsible for our body, which is a "temple of God" (I Cor. 3 : 16). Being responsible for our body means to be responsible for its health. This includes cleanliness.

What would you say if someone would argue: "Since there is no commandment in the Bible which tells us to wash ourselves, we should just 'let nature take its course' and trust in God that he will take the dirt away?" Or: "Since the Bible does not recommend any specific brand of tooth paste, it is sinful to use any at all"?

Once a bus driver had an accident because he didn't put on brakes when going down hill. Several passengers were killed. Could he have excused himself by saying, "I am not permitted to put on brakes, because it is not expressly commanded in the Bible"?

The Bible commands, "Love your neigbour as yourself" (Luke 10 : 27). This means that we are responsible for our neighbour's life. Observing the traffic rules is one way to protect this life. Therefore the driver sinned by n o t putting on the brakes, even though there is nothing written in the Bible about automobile brakes and their use.

I admit, you arrive at this only by way of conclusion. But why did God give us our brains, if not to draw conclusions?

Let's take the example of Kenya. In 1969, its population was about 9 million. The annual rate of increase is 3 per cent. This means that Kenya's population doubles every 23 years. In 92 years it would be multiplied by 16 and reach 144 million in less than a century.[1]

Similar numbers can be given about most of the other African countries. Africa is expected to have the fastest growth rate in the world. Its population is going to double every generation. The danger is that this may wreck all the progress Africa achieves. "Family planning does not solve all problems, but without it, solution of many of them in Africa as elsewhere is impossible."[2]

1) „Family Planning in Kenya", p. 3, Report published by the Ministry of Economic Planning and Development, Nairobi.

2) I. P. P. F. "The Role of Family Planning in African Development", p. 8 and 68.

Now a brief word about the case of Onan in Genesis 38. First of all, this passage does not refer to masturbation.[1] Onan did not masturbate, but used the same method as you did first — the "coitus abruptus".

Nonetheless he was not punished for using conception control, but for his sinful and egoistic motive. He was supposed to give a child to Tamar, his late brother's wife. But this child would not have belonged to him and would not have borne his name. "Onan knew that the offspring would not be his". Therefore — he spilled the semen on the ground, "lest he should give offspring to his brother." When God slew him, he punished Onan's selfishness. This passage has nothing whatsoever to say about God's will concerning responsible parenthood.

As I said before, it is the motive which counts in God's eyes. If your motive is unselfish, you have the liberty of choosing the method which serves your marriage best.

Why didn't I mention condoms? Well, I thought you knew about them and had your reasons for not using them. You see, Joseph, the difficulty in corresponding with you is that you have so many wrong ideas. For example you say: "sperm kills the baby", "pills are poison", "milk makes babies sick", "condoms are only for use with

1) On masturbation see My Parents Are Impossible. — My Beautiful Feeling.

46

prostitutes". Strong emotions are connected with these ideas. I may succeed in convincing you in your head that these ideas are untrue, but that still doesn't change the feelings they cause in your heart.

Your reaction concerning condoms is what I expected. You certainly made a blunder in your classroom. Brother, you missed a unique chance to teach your students a lesson in sex education and at the same time to win their confidence! I am afraid they will hesitate to ask you any questions again for fear of being punished.

The basic rule in sex education is: Answer every question that a child asks immediately, honestly and naturally, regardless of when, where and why the question is asked.

My own children often ask these questions at the dinner table, usually when we have guests. If I would hush them or show any embarrassment, I would give them the impression that sexual matters are sinful, and just in this way make them interesting and attractive. That's why I think by refusing to answer your students, you lead them much more into temptation than by giving them a true and simple explanation.

What a chance to point out to them the difference when contraceptives are used in marital or extramarital situations! The safety risks and apparent inconveniences of physical and psychological nature are certainly much greater in extramarital and especially also in premarital situations.

You will find that young people are very open to this truth if you confront them with facts. From counseling, my impression is that the condom is used relatively seldom by unmarried young people. A medical doctor in charge of the public health program of a large American city confirmed this. One of the reasons is probably that the condom can only be put on when the male organ is in a state of erection. Thus the love play has to be interrupted and this disturbs the spontaneity which characterizes young romance.

For me this is just one more evidence that according to divine will, sex should be an expression of m a r i t a l love. For in marriage both partners can prepare to cope with these difficulties much more easily.

Here, Joseph, you have to use your own imagination and reasoning. You — and especially your good wife.

January 2

Dear Pastor T.,

For more than a year now you have not heard from me. I am sure that you were worried and I apologize very much that I have not answered your last letter. There were two reasons for my silence. The first is that for some time now, Jeannette and

I have been quite happy in our marriage and we did not have any special problems. The second is that about six months ago we moved away from our village, because I was appointed to teach at a school in a larger town. You may have written to me, but the mail probably was not forwarded.

When I say, we have been quite happy, I really mean it. Shortly after we received your last letter we agreed to use NFP. Jeannette made a real effort to watch the symptoms as you explained them in your letter of July 6th. I put a small calendar up in our room. On it she marked an X each month on the day when her period started and M on the days when she felt the wetness from her vagina and mucus. This way I could check too, without her having to tell me.

During the days of "wetness" we abstained from having intercourse and then waited after the mucus had ceased for three more days to be sure that the fertile time was past.

Of course Jeannette did not reach her climax all the time. But as soon as she was sure that she c o u l d succeed and that I tried to help her to reach full satisfaction, she changed her attitude entirely and became "obedient", but not as a maid or a slave as I had expected when I first wrote you. It was a different kind of obedience. How can I describe it?

I got the impression that she almost seemed to like it when I gave her "orders". Sometimes she even asked me of her own accord whether I wanted something or did even more than I asked of her. It was an obedience not out of forced submission but out of willful cooperation.

But now, as you imagine because I write to you again, we have different problems. There are two of them.

The first is money. We never had a money problem as long as we lived in the village. But now we do.

In the village we had a garden and Jeannette fed our family from what she raised. She could sell some of her vegetables at the market and with that money she bought meat, oil, salt and sugar. We also had some chickens and a few goats. I never gave her cash and she never asked for it.

Here in town we have no garden. Neither can we keep animals. Jeannette has to buy every bit of food that we use. There is a large supermarket not far from here and in this store are thousands of cartons and cans with every imaginable kind of food product.

When Jeannette goes into this store it doesn't take her more than ten minutes to spend all the money which I have given her for the whole month. She buys many things which we do not need. Often she buys more food than we can eat, so that it spoils after a few days.

This often leads to new quarrels between us. What can I do to make her buy the right things and to prevent her from spending more money than she can afford? How can you teach a wife to keep her budget?

But there's a second problem too. Please don't laugh at me now! After our long correspondence, it is hard for me to share it. We now have the opposite problem from what I first wrote about.

When we moved to this town our child was already two years old. That's why we decided about six months ago that we would like to have another baby, especially since powdered milk is available here.

Now we want another baby very badly, but it doesn't come! Every time Jeannette has her period she cries, because this means that she is not pregnant. What can we do? She has already had a medical examination, but the doctor could find nothing wrong. What is the reason for infertility?

P. S. from Jeannette: My husband let me read this letter. I think he exaggerated a little bit. Ten minutes are not enough for me to spend all our money in the supermarket. I need at least thirty.

January 27

Dear Joseph and Jeannette,

I was very happy to hear from you again after such a long time. I took your silence as a good sign that you were happy and therefore I didn't worry too much.

Jeannette seems to have developed into an artist of love. Congratulations! I am now convinced all the more that we should publish parts of our correspondence. I wish that many women would read your last letter. Or still better, that many husbands would read it to their wives.

As I said before, every method of contraception involves some handicap to the fellowship of love. If this is true within marriage, it is even more true outside of marriage. The advocates of "free sex" are usually strangely silent about this fact.

In his book on marriage, Dr. Bovet closes the discussion about contraceptives with the following paragraph:

"I must end with a solemn word of warning. We must often be thankful for contraceptives, but the great danger in using these technical things lies in the failure to realize the inherent problem — in other words, using them quite arbitrarily and ignoring the profound association God has once and for all established between sexual union and procreation."

This leads to your questions about infertility. But first let me say a word about your budget problem.

The humorous P. S. of Jeannette shows me that you have also started to share the letters you write. Since you know how to share your problems you are not any more overcome by them. Sharing problems means to divide them into halves.

Sharing money means also to divide it up. You must first of all get away from the idea that you, Joseph, earn the money and that Jeannette spends it. In marriage you have become one flesh. This means that all the money belongs to both of you and you are both equally responsible for the way it is spent.

Therefore Jeannette has to know exactly how much you earn and you must agree on a family budget which you divide up together each month. Some couples pray before they do this.

First you take out your tithe for God. The rest you may divide up into four main parts: clothing, housing, food and emergencies.

The amount for food is taken care of by Jeannette. But you have to be patient with her and not blame her for making mistakes. She has never learned how to handle cash, so you have to teach her. Maybe you should go along a few times when she goes shopping and help her decide what to buy and what not to buy. Jeannette is an intelligent woman. I am sure that after two or three months she will be an expert shopper.

It is also very important that you include in your budget a certain amount of spending money for each of you. Yes, Joseph, you read right. Jeannette, too, should have some pocket money of her own for which she doesn't need to give an account.

Money certainly shouldn't play a major part in our lives. But we have to be realists and recognize the fact that it plays a very important minor part. Hidden feelings of hostility and rivalry in marriage often show up through the medium of money problems. Therefore it is right to deal with them consciously.

In your first letter to me you used the expression "the person I married". The word "person" had a somewhat degrading meaning in your statement. But the real meaning of "person" is very deep. To treat someone as a "person" means to recognize in him the image of God. If you really want to be married to a "person", show this, among many other things, by giving Jeannette her own spending money.

But you can show it too, by allowing her to become again a mother. I am so glad that you are thinking of having another baby. I thought already last year that if you were only willing to boil your milk, you could have had another child long ago. But it was not up to me to make this decision. It was up to you and your wife — before God.

If you now have to wait longer than you planned, it should remind you anew of the fact that children are a gift of God. They are an answer to prayer, a special blessing which God can refuse or give, just as he pleases. He is the Creator, not we.

However, just as God can use a doctor's advice to heal someone from sickness, so also can he use medical help to remove the causes of infertility. There are many causes. J. G. C. Blacker of the United Nations Economic Commission for Africa says: "Infertility is due to physiological causes, possibly the high instance of indigenous malaria, possibly forms of malnutrition and above all probably to high incidences of venereal diseases."

It's good that Jeannette had a medical checkup. But it would not hurt if you would have one too, Joseph. Many ignore the fact that the husband can also be the cause of a childless marriage. It is foolish for husbands to refuse to be examined while they blame their wives for barrenness.

However, in your case, it is very unlikely that there is a medical reason, since you already have a child which was born normally and since you have remained faithful to each other. Therefore let me give you some hints.

You can use Natural Family Planning not to prevent, but to favor conception. You could make it a point to come together on the fertile days when the ovum is released from the ovary. Some doctors give this advice: abstain from intercourse a few days before the fertile days begin and then have intercourse three or four nights in a row in order to give the male semen the maximum power.

Though female orgasm is not absolutely necessary to conception, it seems to favour it.

Still, dear Joseph and Jeannette, all this is only human talking. God may make use of our human wisdom, techniques and tools — or he may not. This is entirely up to him. If he does not want to use them and give you another child of your own, you always have, of course, the possibility of adopting an orphan and in this way, of providing a home for a child who otherwise would have none. Still an adopted child is not the same as your own child. If God does not give you another child of your own, you will have to accept it and love each other just the same.

You made a very profound statement in your last letter, Joseph. You said that Jeannette has become obedient "not out of forced submission, but out of willful cooperation". I have never heard anyone else put in such clear and simple words what the apostle Paul must have meant when he wrote: "Wives, be subject to your husbands, a s to the Lord" (Ephesians 5 : 22). But he also admonished the husbands to love their wives "as Christ loved the church", in other words, unconditionally, including their short-comings.[1]

Therefore, if the Lord does not want to give you another child of your own, you will have to accept it in the same attitude as Elkanah did.

He had a wife called Hannah, but the Lord had "closed her womb". Her rival provoked her sorely and irritated her. Hannah wept and would not eat. Then Elkanah comforted her with the following words:

"Hannah, why do you weep? And why do you not eat? And why is your heart sad? A m I no t m o re to you than ten sons?" (I Sam. 1 : 8).
Elkanah acted that way because "h e l o v e d H a n n a h" (v. 5).

1) See also "I Loved a Girl", letter of Aug. 3rd.